contents

juices and smoothies in sport

Natural juices and smoothies are great for sports people because they deliver fluid, energy-giving carbohydrate, and a wealth of other important nutrients all in one glass. They are quick and easy to prepare but, unlike most fast foods, they contain no artificial sweeteners, preservatives, or other chemicals. The good news is that they will give a beneficial boost before, during, and particularly after exercise (see page 19), a time when athletes can lose their appetite for solid food.

The need for fluid and carbohydrate is so important when exercising that it is better to consume carbohydrate in a less bulky, lower-fiber form, which makes it quicker and easier to absorb. Juices and smoothies fit the bill because they provide fluid and carbohydrate while being low in fiber. This is also convenient for athletes who have little time for eating and do not want too much bulky food when exercising—a juice is quick to drink and light on the stomach.

key points
- Juices and smoothies provide valuable fluid, carbohydrate, vitamins (particularly the antioxidant vitamins C and E), and minerals.
- They provide vital nutrition before, during, and after exercise—a particularly important time as the athlete may not be able to tolerate solid food.
- They are low in fat and in fiber (fiber slows carbohydrate absorption).
- Juices and smoothies can be high or low in energy as you wish, depending on your physical needs.
- Juices and smoothies are tasty, easy to make, and ideal when time is limited.

- Homemade juices pack a nutritional punch. Not only do you avoid the vitamin and mineral losses that occur during cooking, but homemade juices are also free from preservatives, sweeteners, and other chemicals, and provide a concentrated and easily absorbed source of vitamins and minerals.

Juicing basics
- Buy fruit and vegetables that are in season.
- Choose fruit that is just ripe but not over-ripe.
- Avoid bruised or wilted produce.
- Where possible, buy organic (see page 22).
- Buy fruit and vegetables in small amounts and often.
- Prepare fruit and vegetables just before juicing to retain the vitamins.

juices as supplements
Athletes often wonder what they can take to improve their performance. The use of nutritional supplements or ergogenic (work-producing) aids may help athletes toward their goal by:
- Making up for an inadequate diet or lifestyle.
- Meeting a specific or unusual nutrient requirement resulting from the demands of training and competition.
- Directly affecting sports performance.

A dietary supplement can be:
- Sports drinks
- High-carbohydrate supplements
- Liquid meal supplements
- Sports bars/energy bars
- Vitamin and/or mineral supplements
- Iron supplements
- Calcium supplements

50 nutritious juices for exercise

POWER
JUICES

PENNY HUNKING & FIONA HUNTER

HAMLYN HEALTHY EATING

An Hachette UK Company
www.hachette.co.uk

First published in Great Britain in 2007
by Hamlyn, a division of Octopus Publishing Group Ltd
Endeavour House
189 Shaftesbury Avenue
London
WC2H 8JY
www.octopusbooksusa.com

Revised edition 2010
This edition published in 2014

Distributed in the US by
Hachette Book Group USA
237 Park Avenue
New York, NY 10017 USA

Distributed in Canada by
Canadian Manda Group
165 Dufferin Street
Toronto, Ontario, Canada M6K 3H6

Penny Hunking and Fiona Hunter assert the moral right
to be identified as the authors of this work.

ISBN 978-0-600-62989-4

Printed and bound in China

10 9 8 7 6 5 4 3 2 1

Safety Note

Power Juices should not be considered a replacement for professional medical treatment; a physician should be consulted on all matters relating to health. Athletes and exercisers should seek personal nutrition advice from an appropriately qualified nutrition professional such as an Accredited Sports Dietitian or Registered Nutritionist. While the advice and information in this book is believed to be accurate, neither the authors nor publisher can accept any legal responsibility for any injury or illness sustained while following the advice in this book.

Ergogenic aids contain nutrients in amounts greater than the recommended daily intake (RDI) and suggest or claim a direct effect on sports performance. Yet there is little documented scientific support for many of these products. Some nutritional supplements do have a role in helping athletes train and perform better, but they can never be a substitute for a well-planned diet and training program, adequate rest and recovery, and good mental preparation.

Making fresh juices and smoothies an integral part of your daily training diet, they will not only have a positive effect on your sports performance because of their high carbohydrate and fluid content, they will also contribute to your overall good health due to their high nutritional value.

which fruit and vegetables are best for athletes?

Recent research has shown that some have a higher oxygen radical absorbency capacity (ORAC) than others. This measures their antioxidant potential—in other words, their ability to neutralize the damaging free radicals that can cause cancer and heart disease. Fruit with the highest ORAC are: prunes, blueberries, blackberries, strawberries, raisins, raspberries, oranges, plums, black grapes, and cherries. Vegetables with the highest ORAC are: kale, red sweet peppers, Brussels sprouts, garlic, corn, spinach, onions, broccoli, eggplants, and alfalfa.

sports nutrition

The right diet combined with proper training significantly improves athletic performance, whether it's a Sunday morning soccer match or running a marathon. Exercise puts extra demands on the body—athletes need more energy, lose more body fluid and have extra stresses on muscles, bones, and joints. Dietary changes can significantly affect training and recovery at every level. However, nutritional requirements vary widely—those who regularly train for more than one hour each day have different needs from those who enjoy a team match once a week.

micronutrients of significant importance

Micronutrient	Function	Benefit to the athlete
Calcium	Bone/tooth structure. Helps muscle contraction, nerve transmission, secretion of hormones, digestive enzymes, and neurotransmitters	Adequate calcium intake plus exercise prevents bone loss. Good bone health is essential and athletes need to be free from stress fractures and serious bone injury
Iron	Red blood cell formation. Transport of oxygen. Helps immune function	Iron deficiency can impair performance. Exercise can destroy red blood cells, so sports people are likely to need more iron in their diet. Female athletes are particularly at risk because of menstrual blood losses
Vitamin A (retinol)	Essential for vision. Protects mucous membranes lining the nose, mouth, and throat, and so prevents bronchitis	Good vision is important to everyone, particularly sports people and those who train in low light
Vitamin C (ascorbic acid)	Growth and repair of cells and tissues. Promotes healthy blood vessels, gums, and teeth. Powerful antioxidant	Exercise may increase vitamin C requirement. Vitamin C may help prevent cancer and heart disease
Vitamin E	Powerful antioxidant, protects from free radical damage	Protects cells from damage. Exercisers may need more than non-exercisers
Magnesium	Involved in muscle contraction and formation of new cells. Assists in energy production. Part of structure of bones	May play important role in aerobic metabolism
Zinc	Helps immunity. Involved in wound healing, metabolism of carbohydrates, proteins, and fats. Vegetarian diets may be deficient in zinc	Adequate intake is important as sports people with a deficiency may have an impaired immune system
B vitamins	Red blood cell formation. Energy release from carbohydrates. Manufacture of hormones and antibodies. Metabolism of fats and proteins. Normal functioning of nerves, brain, and muscles	May have increased needs related to energy production. Also involved in red blood cell formation so protects against anemia

So how do we know what to eat? Energy intake generally increases during exercise, so food and drink choices must reflect this, while regulating the body's intake of macronutrients (protein, fat, and carbohydrate) and micronutrients (vitamins, minerals, and trace elements). There are about 20 different vitamins, most of which must be obtained from the diet. Vitamins A, D, E, K, and B12 can be stored by the body; the rest need to be provided by the diet on a regular basis.

With the right food choices, most exercisers will automatically get more than enough nutrients in their diet. Juices and smoothies are a quick and easy way of ensuring a greater intake of essential nutrients, benefiting energy levels and long-term good health.

To acknowledge this link between diet and athletic performance, a whole new area of nutrition—sports nutrition—has evolved. Sports nutrition has been defined as: "The influence of nutrition on human performance during the preparation for, the participation in and the recovery from sport and exercise." (Professor Clyde Williams, Loughborough University, UK.)

The main aims of sports nutrition are to help the athlete avoid fatigue, dehydration, and poor performance, and to optimize his or her energy levels—the greater the intensity of the exercise, the greater the reliance on carbohydrate as a fuel. The two key issues are, therefore, carbohydrate intake and fluid intake.

Good sources

Milk, yogurt, cheese, canned fish with bones, baked beans, dried figs, oranges, apricots, green vegetables, sesame seeds, almonds, Brazil nuts
Red meat, liver, lentils, fortified breakfast cereals, green leafy vegetables, figs, dates, beans, dark poultry meat
Liver, eggs, meat, whole milk, cheese, oily fish, margarine
Fruit and vegetables, particularly kiwifruit, citrus fruit, red sweet peppers, strawberries, and black currants
Whole wheat bread, cereals, egg yolk, nuts, avocado, sunflower seeds
Fruit and vegetables, milk, potatoes, cereals
Milk and dairy products, eggs, meat, wholegrain cereals
Many, including brown rice, liver, nuts, eggs, beans, green vegetables, bread, cereals, meat, chicken, turkey, variety meats, wheatgerm

the principles of sports nutrition

- **To provide basic nutrient requirements**
- **To promote long-term good health**
- **To achieve and maintain appropriate levels of body mass and body fat**
- **To promote optimal recovery from training sessions**
- **To support training sessions**
- **To create opportunities to try out new eating and drinking practices**

eat five

Current guidelines recommend at least five portions of fruit and vegetables every day.
A portion equals:

- 1 apple, pear, orange, peach, nectarine, or banana
- 2 plums or kiwifruit
- 1 large slice of melon or pineapple
- 1 small glass (⅔ cup) fruit juice
- 2–3 tablespoons vegetables
- 1 dessert bowl of salad

vegetarian athletes

Vegetarians—whether they are athletes or not—usually have high-carbohydrate diets (bread, rice, pasta, cereals, potatoes, and legumes). Vegetarian diets can be healthy since many vegetarians have a lower saturated fat intake than non-vegetarians. However, unless a vegetarian diet is balanced, it can lead to a deficiency in iron, vitamin B12, calcium, zinc, and protein, so these nutrients are crucial.

the importance of carbohydrate

Carbohydrates are essential for optimum athletic performance, and the great news is that juices and smoothies are an excellent way to help you obtain the amount of carbohydrate you need every day.

After digestion, carbohydrate is either circulated in the blood as glucose where it is available for instant use, or stored in the liver and muscles as glycogen. Fatigue is associated with depletion of glycogen stores, so athletes must eat sufficient carbohydrate to train and compete effectively. The body stores only small amounts of carbohydrate and these decrease with any activity. It is important, therefore, to restock glycogen stores after training or you will experience a feeling of heavy legs and tiredness, particularly in endurance training.

Sources of carbohydrate

Sports people are usually told that they should eat more bread, rice, pasta, cereals, and potatoes to get the energy they need, yet beans, lentils, fruit, some vegetables, and dairy foods such as milk and yogurt also provide good levels of carbohydrate. Different sports place different demands on the participant, so food and drink should be matched to individual requirements (see page 14).

Glycemic index

The glycemic index ranks foods according to their effect on blood sugar—a food with a high glycemic index causes blood sugar to rise more quickly than a food with a low glycemic index.

Consumed after exercise, a high glycemic index food will help to replace glycogen more quickly and may be useful during sport. A low glycemic index food eaten before exercise, on the other hand, can provide a slow release of energy and help delay fatigue. Juices and smoothies vary in their glycemic indices, depending upon the recipe and type of fruit and vegetables used (see individual recipes).

Foods with a high glycemic index include: glucose, baked potato, watermelon, white bagels, honey, and cornflakes.

Foods with a low glycemic index include: milk, yogurt, oats, heavy-grain bread, apples, pears, plums, oranges, and lentils.

How much carbohydrate do athletes need?

This varies, depending on the type of exercise, its duration, how often it is performed, and body weight.

For weight maintenance, sedentary people require 4.5 g of carbohydrate per kilogram (2¼ lb) of body weight each day; active people require up to 10 g of carbohydrate per kilogram of body weight each day.

To determine your own carbohydrate needs, multiply your weight in kilograms (kg) by the appropriate amount of carbohydrate per kg from the table below. For example, a female athlete weighing 50 kg and training for more than one hour every day would require at least 300 g of carbohydrate daily (50 x 6 = 300 g).

fat

While some fat is essential in the diet— it provides the body with nine calories of energy per gram, plus the fat-soluble vitamins A, D, E, and K—athletes should keep their fat intake to 30 percent or less of their total calorie consumption. It is carbohydrate availability, not fat, that influences physical performance.

protein

Protein is needed for growth, repair and renewal of tissues, and reproduction. Each gram of protein provides the body with four calories of energy, so proteins also provide energy when carbohydrates and fats are in short supply. Due to their increased energy intake and thus overall amount of food eaten, most athletes consume enough extra protein to compensate for their exercise.

The protein requirement for adults is 0.8 g of protein per kilogram of body weight per day. Animal proteins (such as meat, poultry, fish, cheese, eggs, milk, and yogurt) are often quite high in fat. Vegetable proteins (such as peas, beans, lentils, bread, rice, cereals, and potatoes), however, have a higher carbohydrate content and also provide energy. Other good sources of protein include nuts, seeds, and soy products such as milk, cheese and yogurt.

carbohydrate requirements of athletes

Training hours each day	Carbohydrate per kg (2¼ lb) body weight needed per day
less than 1 hour	4–5 g
1–2 hours	6–7 g
more than 3 hours	8–10 g

fluid

A good fluid intake is essential for health and athletic performance—even mild dehydration can cause fatigue and affect performance. Start exercise well hydrated, drink fluids during exercise, and replace fluids after exercise.

fluid losses

The amount of fluid lost during exercise depends on various factors, including the outside temperature, clothing, and the intensity and duration of the exercise. In some activities, such as weight-training, glycogen is lost from the working muscle but the sweat rate may be quite low. Fluid and glycogen replacement becomes a priority when the recovery rate must be fast, for example, during competition over several days (particularly in the heat).

Fluid losses are measured as weight losses. Every kilogram (2¼ lb) of body weight lost during exercise reflects a loss of about (2½ pints) of fluid which must be replaced. A two percent loss of body weight can affect performance and a four percent loss of body weight can cause exhaustion. To determine how much has been lost, athletes should weigh themselves before and after exercise (preferably almost naked as sweat-soaked clothes are heavy) then compare results. To calculate your percentage body weight loss use this formula:

pre-exercise weight – post-exercise weight / pre-exercise weight x 100 = percentage weight lost

For example:

60 kg – 58.5 kg = 1.5 kg
1.5 kg / 60 kg x 100 = 2.5 percent

what type of fluid?

Electrolytes are mineral salts that are dissolved in the body's fluids and are vital to help athletes maintain the water balance in their bodies. They also help muscles to contract and relax and transmit nerve impulses. To improve performance and to rehydrate after exercise, drinks that contain carbohydrate together with electrolytes, particularly sodium, are more effective than water alone. This is because they decrease urine production and aid fast rehydration and refueling of glycogen stores. So drinks which contain electrolytes may be a better choice than plain water, especially for athletes who sweat heavily. Drinks fall into three categories—hypotonic, isotonic, and hypertonic.

the amount of fluid you need depends on:

- Length of the training session (more sweat is likely to be lost)
- Intensity of the training session (sweat rates are higher as the intensity rises)
- Acclimatization (exercising in a new environment places extra demands on sweat rates)
- Size (larger people may need to drink more fluid)
- Clothing (wearing more clothes may increase the sweat rate)
- The climate (the hotter the temperature, the more the athlete will sweat)
- Environmental conditions—athletes may not notice how much sweat they are losing on wet or windy days

Hypotonic

Less concentrated than the body's fluids, these are quickly absorbed so they are useful both before and during exercise. Hypotonic drinks usually contain less than 4 g of carbohydrate in ½ cup fluid.

Isotonic

These have the same concentration of dissolved particles as the body's fluids and usually contain 4–8 g of carbohydrate in ½ cup. They can be drunk before, during, and after exercise and are generally considered the best choice because they provide the exerciser with fluid and carbohydrate, yet are rapidly absorbed by the body. They can rehydrate and offset potential dehydration better than hypotonic drinks. In addition, they supplement the body's limited carbohydrate stores and can improve exercise performance as well as preventing dehydration.

Hypertonic

These drinks have a higher concentration of dissolved particles than the body's fluids and are absorbed quite slowly, so are usually recommended after exercise when fluid replacement is not a priority. A hypertonic drink contains more than 8 g of carbohydrate in ½ cup.

key points

Hypotonic and isotonic drinks are absorbed quickly, so are useful when fast rehydration is needed usually before or during exercise. Hypertonic drinks are absorbed more slowly so these are a better choice when recovery can be slower and the priority is glycogen replacement, particularly if the athlete does not feel hungry. This is very important to remember when choosing a juice or smoothie for sports performance.

are you getting enough?

- **The average person should drink at least 8 cups of fluid a day. Athletes are likely to need much more than this**
- **Keep a fluid diary**
- **Drink regularly from a water bottle**
- **Implement fluid-intake strategies in training and do not try anything new in competition**
- **Look at your urine—if it is pale or clear, you are well hydrated. The darker it is, the more dehydrated you are. If it is dark orange, drink plenty of fluid immediately**

nutrition for long-term good health

Athletes need to keep up fluid and energy levels day to day, but they also need to think about their health in the long term. Exercise strengthens bones, but too much exercise and too little of the right food can seriously damage bones, particularly in women. Juices and smoothies provide many of the vitamins and minerals essential for long-term good health. Nutrition experts worldwide agree that fruit and vegetables are the cornerstones of a healthy diet—in Mediterranean countries, where fruit and vegetables form a large part of the diet, people are generally healthier. It is also known that fruit and vegetables can help protect against cancer, heart disease, and many other health problems.

calcium

Essential for good bone health and also involved in nerve transmission, blood clotting, and muscle function, calcium is found in milk and most dairy products, green leafy vegetables, canned fish with bones, nuts, seeds, and fortified soy products such as tofu. The absorption of calcium is aided by vitamin D, which our bodies produce by the action of sunlight on the skin.

Most of the juices in this book will boost calcium intake. Smoothies made with milk, yogurt, and ice cream are very helpful for athletes as this calcium is easily available.

Adequate calcium intake reduces the risk of osteoporosis, which can occur in young women, particularly if they over-exercise and are underweight with low body fat.

iron

An adequate intake of iron is essential for all athletes, particularly females. Iron makes hemoglobin in the red blood cells that carry oxygen around the body. Even a marginal deficiency of iron can leave athletes too tired to train and recover effectively, with symptoms of severe fatigue, cramps, headaches, and shortness of breath. Iron can be lost through sweat, gastro-intestinal bleeding, and jarring during contact sports. Athletes who restrict how much they eat put themselves at a higher risk of developing iron deficiency.

athletes most at risk from calcium deficiency

- Women
- Vegetarians and vegans
- Those who are underweight or have low body fat
- Those who have poor food/energy (kilocalorie) intake
- Women who are not menstruating
- Those who over-train

athletes most at risk from iron deficiency

- Women
- Vegetarians and vegans
- Faddy eaters and those making poor food choices
- Those following a low or restricted energy intake
- Those eating many high-carbohydrate foods
- Those in heavy-endurance training

Iron also helps in the synthesis of enzymes, forms part of the myoglobin in muscle cells, and helps immune function. Iron from animal sources (red meat, for example) is absorbed in the body more easily than iron from vegetable sources, such as spinach. Iron absorption can be increased by eating foods rich in vitamin C (see recipes and Top Ingredients for Power Juices, page 20) at the same time as the iron-rich foods. Iron deficiency is easily preventable by eating more iron-rich foods (green leafy vegetables, for example).

Sports anemia

Sports anaemia, characterized by tiredness, is caused by an increased volume of blood in the body at the start of physical activity and means that iron is, in effect, more diluted in the blood. Performance is not generally affected, so if tiredness continues it is more likely to be due to a true lack of iron in the diet or another aspect of training. Self-diagnosis is not advised; if tiredness continues, see your doctor.

female athlete triad

This refers to three inter-related conditions: disordered eating, amenorrhea (lack of menstruation), and osteoporosis. Some female athletes and non-athletes do not consider that training or exercise is sufficient to achieve their ideal body shape. Consequently, a significant number use harmful practices such as restricted eating, vomiting, laxatives and diuretics to lose weight and shape up. These may lead to menstrual dysfunction, which in turn may cause reduced bone density and osteoporosis. Every portion of the triad increases the chance of ill health and death, but the dangers are synergistic.

Prevention is the only long-term solution: make sure you eat a healthy balanced diet that is sufficient in energy and contains a variety of foods.

nutritional needs for different sports

Each type of physical exercise has specific nutritional needs. For example, someone playing tennis is likely to use more energy playing singles, rather than doubles, and a racing cyclist will expend more calories than someone on a social cycle ride. Similarly a goalkeeper is likely to use less energy in a socer match than a striker. Team players' nutritional needs must also support the demands of training.

Whatever your sport, and whatever level you practice at, juices and smoothies are the perfect nutritional aid.

aerobic exercise

Aerobic exercise is any repetitive, relatively low-intensity, and rhythmical exercise involving the large muscle groups such as the quadriceps (thigh muscles). Aerobic means "with oxygen"; aerobic exercise adds to the workload of the heart and lungs as the body increases its need for oxygen. Aerobic activities include:
• Fitness classes/aerobic dancing • Running
• Swimming • Cycling (leisure) • Power walking • Social dancing

Fitness classes/aerobic dancing Many people participate in fitness classes at all levels, mainly to get fit and lose weight. It is important, however, that exercisers do not fall into the trap of not eating after the class because they do not want to replace the calories they have just used. A juice or smoothie with a low-fat, high-carbohydrate meal or snack consumed within one to two hours of the class is ideal.

Running Runners often strive to achieve a low level of body fat and the quantity, type,

and timing of food and fluid consumed can sometimes be of concern.

Swimming It is easy to dehydrate and not notice when swimming. Isotonic drinks can be left at the end of the lane for frequent drinks. Swimmers often carry a little extra body fat: this protects them from getting chilly in the water and aids buoyancy.

Cycling (leisure) Cyclists can lose quite a lot of fluid without realizing it, particularly in hot or windy weather. A feeder bottle can be carried on the bike.

Power walking Don your walking shoes, wear comfortable clothes, and off you go! Carry a drink with you and take regular sips.

Social dancing Fluid losses can be quite high so take regular breaks to drink. If you are drinking alcohol, juices and smoothies can help to offset the dehydration that often occurs with alcohol (in addition to fluid lost through dancing).

endurance activities

Endurance activities are generally defined as 90 minutes or more of continuous, high-intensity exercise. Endurance activities include:
• Long-distance running • Triathlon • Rowing
• Competition swimming • Cross-country running • Cycling (racing)

Long-distance running This area of sport, which includes marathons, poses a huge nutritional challenge. It is vital that athletes keep their fluid intake high and replenish glucose and electrolytes. If running for more than one hour, runners should drink at least 2 cups of liquid per hour, or more when the weather is hot. Isotonic drinks are a good choice.

Triathlon Participants complete a swim, cycle, and a run in succession. Triathletes strive for low levels of body fat and focus on high-carbohydrate, low-fat meals, snacks, and drinks. Juices and smoothies are ideal on a daily basis.

Rowing Rowers need enormous amounts of energy and carbohydrate to support intense training loads, often eight to ten months of the year and up to 12 times a week. They need to eat well-balanced, nutritious food as frequently as possible to ensure that they take in enough calories.

Competition swimming Competitions can last for up to a week, with swimmers in and out of the water all day. Good recovery is crucial and the key issues are hydration and the refueling of muscle glycogen stores.

Cross-country running As with any long-distance running, runners must start well fueled and well hydrated and eat and drink as they go. Cross-country runners need to plan well and may need to carry fluids and snacks with them.

Cycling (racing) Racing cyclists train long and hard. They must eat a high-energy, well-balanced diet, which is high in protein, vitamins, minerals, and carbohydrate. Calorie needs can be huge so cyclists must eat and drink frequently, even while cycling. Sweat losses can be very high, so fluid replacement is essential, especially on hotter, windy, and more humid days.

low-intensity exercise

Many different sports and activities can be performed at varying intensities—defined by how hard the individual is working. Low-intensity exercise typically includes:
- Walking at a moderate pace • Golf
- Cricket • Scuba diving

Walking Moderate walking requires less energy than power walking and running. A well-balanced diet should be eaten at all times and walkers should pay particular attention to their fluid intake.

Golf Golfers need to concentrate over long periods of time and may be under a degree of nervous stress. As a result, balance and coordination are likely to suffer, so they should frequently consume carbohydrate-containing fluids and snacks.

Cricket Cricketers can be out on the pitch for many hours and should start play well fueled and well hydrated. All cricketers should drink as frequently as possible.

Scuba diving Scuba diving (sport diving) poses particular challenges in food and fluid intake. Body heat is lost 25 times faster under water than in air, and scuba divers can easily experience hypothermia and need plenty of energy. Urine production is increased, so divers must drink copious amounts of fluid directly before and after a dive.

extra-energy sports

Athletes performing these sports must start well fueled, well hydrated, and with plenty of glycogen in their muscles. This means they must eat well in the day and hours before playing. Some sports have a very definite time frame; others, such as tennis, do not.

Fluid needs are high, particularly on hot days. Extra-energy sports include:
• Tennis • Hockey • Football • Rugby • Squash • Circuit training • Full-contact martial arts • Water skiing (competition) • Basketball • Netball

Tennis Food and drink can be consumed between sets. Fluid needs can be very high and it is vital to drink as often as possible. Isotonic drinks are best: they replace lost fluids quickly and provide extra energy in the form of carbohydrate.

Hockey Recovery between matches is difficult, particularly with a heavy training load, and players must pay special attention to their intake of carbohydrate and fluid every day of the week. To maintain their weight, players should keep their general nutrient intake well balanced and follow a high-carbohydrate, low-fat eating style.

Football Footballers need a high level of fitness and energy. Some players have higher energy needs than others depending on their role and can experience fatigue quite early in the match. Good nutrition strategies help prevent this. The key is to keep carbohydrate and fluid intake high.

Rugby Forwards require strength and power to help win the ball; backs help to carry the ball forward via their speed and agility to withstand the tackles from the opposition. Causes of fatigue in rugby players can be many—depletion of muscle glycogen stores and dehydration are the most likely.

Squash Squash is very demanding physically, requiring agility, coordination, and good aerobic fitness. A match can last 90 minutes or more, with very high body temperature and sweat rates. Players must start a game well fueled and well hydrated.

Circuit training Very intense exercise in which a group of exercises are completed one after another for a specific length of time. Many athletes use circuit training to complement training in their specific sport. Anyone circuit training should follow the principles of a well-balanced diet at all times.

Full-contact martial arts Training involves short bursts of energy, some of it very intense. Good technique is needed and good concentration is essential. Training sessions are often around two hours and an adequate fluid intake is key, especially among those who use diuretics and saunas for weight control. Athletes practicing this sport may have increased iron needs because of bruising and bleeding from combat injuries.

Water skiing (competition, tricks) An extremely high-energy sport. In essence, water skiers participate in several short intermittent periods of high-intensity exercise. It is vital they eat and drink regularly throughout the day. Fluid needs vary and could be very high on hot days.

Basketball Basketball requires a very high level of skill and fitness. Lower body fat levels can be an advantage to help jumps, speed, and agility. Iron needs are likely to be higher because of the impact involved in contact with other players and impact on the floor. Fluid losses through sweating can be significant, so fluids must be consumed on the court sidelines.

Netball Netballers have similar needs to basketball players. Iron needs may be higher because of the impact from running and jumps. There is increased destruction of red blood cells in athletes with high training loads of high-impact exercise. Fluid needs can be quite high, so fluids must be consumed on the court sidelines.

muscular strength activities

Many elite athletes and recreational exercisers weight-train, and these tough training sessions must be supported by high-energy intakes of carbohydrate. Protein is not as suitable as it is commonly thought since it is not converted into muscle, simply into extra energy to fuel the muscle. This extra energy is better obtained through carbohydrates. Muscle burns calories so athletes with more muscle need plenty of energy. They should eat regularly and keep well hydrated. Juices and smoothies are an ideal way of achieving this.

general fitness activities

What is fitness? It is a relative term with many health-related and skill-related components. Health-related components include muscular strength and endurance, aerobic fitness, and flexibility. Skill-related components include balance, agility, reaction time, speed, power, and coordination. Activities include:
• Gym workouts • Pilates • Yoga
• Body conditioning • Water skiing •
Wakeboarding • Sailing • Roller skating •
Skateboarding • Semi-contact martial arts
• Hiking • Ice skating • Playing with a
Frisbee • Housework, gardening, washing
the car • Walking the dog

17

eating and competing

Anyone who exercises regularly must follow a well-balanced, nutrient-dense diet, matching energy intake and expenditure to achieve a consistent weight. Fluid intake is of key importance: even a small amount of dehydration affects balance, coordination, agility and concentration, impairs performance, and can lead to fatigue.

What the athlete actually needs in theory may be difficult to achieve in practice. Carbohydrate and fluid intakes are the most important considerations and juices and smoothies can deliver both at the same time and in an easily tolerated form. The key to eating and competing is to practice different eating and drinking strategies until you find one that suits you personally. Do not try anything new "on the day" or you could experience a few undesirable side effects!

before the event

Some athletes can eat and compete, some cannot. The pre-event meal—two to three hours beforehand—should be high in carbohydrate and low in fat and should be easy to digest so the stomach is left empty for the event. Remember that liquid meals will empty from the stomach quickly, so you may need more to sustain yourself over a longer period of time. Ask yourself the following questions:

- Does the event involve running, jumping, or physical contact?
  If so, leave a little longer between eating and competing.
- Is your body supported—for example, cycling, swimming, and rowing? If so, you may be able to eat nearer the event.
- Will you get an attack of nerves?
  If so, eat a little earlier.

during the event

Nutritional and fluid needs vary widely, although studies show that carbohydrate intake during prolonged exercise lasting longer than 90 minutes enhances performance. Fluid intake before, during, and after an event is a priority. Juices and smoothies are very useful because they:

- Taste good, so more is likely to be drunk.
- Are easy to absorb.
- Deliver some carbohydrate to help improve endurance and delay fatigue.

Unfortunately, many athletes suffer from nausea, vomiting, and diarrhea during competitive events. Problems often relate to the pre-event meal, so juices and smoothies may be more suitable than solid food.

Factors that can increase the risk of problems are:
- Poor training
- Dehydration
- Nervousness
- Being female
- High-intensity exercise
- Running and jumping

pre-event juices and smoothies

Juices and smoothies are especially suitable before an event if:
- You are not hungry
- The event starts very early
- The event involves running, jumping, or physical contact
- Fluid replacement is a priority
- It is a hot and/or humid day

Team sports

Most team sports last up to 90 minutes. Players need to start the game with well-fueled muscles, so they should eat plenty of food and drink containing carbohydrate. An isotonic drink will help to replace fluid lost in sweat and provide some carbohydrate to delay fatigue.

Endurance events

Endurance events usually last longer than 90 minutes and so it is important to take on fluid and fuel (carbohydrate) throughout. Smoothies would be ideal here, as they will provide fluid and the extra 30–60 g of carbohydrate needed. When sweat rates are high, choose an isotonic drink.

Ultra-endurance events

These challenging events, such as the Ironman triathlon, usually last over four hours. The athletes compete at a lower intensity, so digestion is often little affected and athletes can eat, drink and digest food and fluids with higher carbohydrate during the event. Smoothies are ideal, together with snacks such as granola bars.

after the event

The athlete may be too exhausted to even think about eating and drinking after competing, yet it is vital to do so as soon as possible—preferably within two hours. Smoothies contain both carbohydrate and protein, and are ideal to help rehydration and refueling of the muscles.

The first meal after exercise should provide at least 1 g of carbohydrate per kilogram (2¼ lb) of body weight. Athletes should also drink at least 2 cups of fluid immediately after competing and continue drinking at regular intervals.

juices versus smoothies?

Smoothies, full of nutrients and a good source of calcium, are usually more filling and a good choice before and immediately after exercise when solid food may not appeal to you. Juices also provide a wealth of nutrients, but are often useful during exercise when fluid needs are higher. Choose an isotonic juice or smoothie when fluid replacement is important.

19

top ingredients for power juices

Apples have a higher antioxidant vitamin content than soft or citrus fruits as they contain a flavonoid called quercetin, thought to be a potent antioxidant. Exercisers may need extra antioxidants to counter the potentially damaging effect of free radicals, produced more freely during exercise.

Apricots, especially dried, are a good source of beta-carotene, potassium, and iron.

Avocados contain more protein than any fruit, and are high in monounsaturated fat. They are a rich source of vitamin E and supply amounts of vitamin C, vitamin B6, potassium, riboflavin, and manganese.

Bananas are especially popular with endurance athletes as they are a great source of carbohydrate and potassium, but are low in fat and sodium. Make sure you choose really ripe ones as unripe bananas are largely indigestible.

Carrots are an excellent source of beta-carotene (made more available by juicing), the plant form of vitamin A, which is crucial for good vision—particularly useful for scuba divers and early-morning runners. High intakes of beta-carotene may also help to fight the damage done by free radicals and so protect against some types of cancer. Carrots can also help lower blood cholesterol levels.

Cranberries—daily consumption of cranberry juice helps to decrease the risk of urinary tract infections (UTIs). Cranberries are also a good source of antioxidant vitamin C and flavonoids.

Grapes are ideal after exercise as they are a good source of potassium. Red and black grapes contain more antioxidants than green ones.

Kiwifruit are naturally high in potassium and vitamin C, which helps to protect athletes from muscle damage, decreases muscle soreness, and accelerates general healing. Vitamin C may also help to increase oxygen uptake and aerobic energy production which is particularly useful for athletes when they are competing:

Lemons are an excellent source of vitamin C, an essential water-soluble vitamin involved in many metabolic processes including those that influence the functioning of the aerobic system. A very powerful antioxidant, vitamin C helps to prevent cellular damage and impairment of the immune system and aids the absorption of dietary iron.

Mangoes are an excellent source of vitamin C and beta-carotene, which is converted into vitamin A, boosting the body's defenses and preventing damage by free radicals.

Melons are low in calories and high in water content. Orange-fleshed melons are a good source of vitamin C and beta-carotene; lighter-colored melons less so.

Watermelons have a high glycemic index, so juices made with this fruit are good after exercise, particularly when fluid replacement is a priority.

Oranges are an excellent source of the antioxidant vitamin C. They also provide folate (important for female athletes) and potassium (vital for muscle and nerve function).

Peaches are an excellent source of vitamin C. They are easily digestible and have a gentle laxative effect.

Pears are a useful source of vitamin C and potassium. They contain natural fruit sugars for extra energy.

Pink grapefruit are a great source of vitamin C, folate (an essential B vitamin), potassium, and lycopene. Folate deficiency

could impair aerobic performance; it is also vital for females of child-bearing age because of its role in the prevention of birth defects.

Plums, particularly dried ones (prunes), contain useful amounts of fiber and are a good source of potassium. They also contain iron.

Purple grape juice contains favorable amounts of antioxidants called bioflavonoids and is a good source of potassium—essential for optimum cell, nerve and muscle function and for regulating blood pressure, and therefore vital for athletic performance.

Red currants are an excellent source of vitamin C and a good source of potassium. They also contain reasonable levels of iron.

Spinach is a great source of beta-carotene (vitamin A) and a fair source of many other nutrients including iron, calcium, folate, and vitamins B1, C and E.

Strawberries are a great source of vitamin C. In addition, they are a fair source of folate, which is also necessary for red blood cell manufacture and so is needed to prevent anemia.

Tomatoes are a good source of vitamin C and the antioxidant, lycopene. Research indicates that people who frequently eat tomatoes and tomato products have a lower risk of certain cancers, particularly prostate cancer, and heart disease, than those who eat them rarely. Tomato-based juices are ideal before and after exercise.

Milk—athletes can achieve their required daily intake of calcium by drinking just 2½ cups of milk daily. Ninety-nine percent of the body's calcium is in the skeleton, making it essential for athletes who need strong, healthy bones. Milk is also a good source of protein, zinc, phosphorus, B vitamins, and vitamin A. Skim milk loses its vitamin A, but is lower in fat than whole milk. Lowfat and skim milk are a better source of calcium than whole milk.

is it nutritionally better to eat organic fruit and vegetables?

Organically grown produce may contain higher levels of vitamins and phytochemicals. But there is another reason for choosing organic produce. Unless you buy organic, you will inevitably increase your intake of pesticide residues. Although the health risks from pesticides are small, the effects of long-term exposure to them are unknown. However, some residues can be removed by thoroughly washing fruit and vegetables.

Quark is a soft curd cheese which is low in fat and is an excellent source of protein, vitamins, and minerals, including calcium.

Soy milk is an alternative to cows' milk for vegan or lactose-intolerant athletes. However, because soy milk naturally lacks calcium, it is better to choose a brand that is fortified with calcium. Soy milk contains about the same amount of protein as cows' milk and there is growing interest in the role that soy plays in men's and women's health.

Yogurt is a great source of calcium. It also has a low glycemic index so is ideal before endurance exercise as well as after any exercise.

Peanut butter—fiber-providing peanuts are more than 25 percent protein and high in fat, although over 75 percent of this is monounsaturated and polyunsaturated, which can help to reduce blood cholesterol levels. Peanut butter is a good source of vitamin E and B vitamins, copper, and magnesium. Peanuts also contain phytochemicals including resveratrol, thought to play a role in protecting against cancer and heart disease.

making perfect juices and smoothies

Refreshing and nutritious, juices and smoothies are quick and easy to prepare and make a great energy booster, snack, or meal replacement. All you need is a sharp knife, a juice extractor, and a blender or food processor.

equipment

If you plan to make both juices and smoothies you will need two machines. For juices you will need a juice extractor, for smoothies you will need a blender or food processor. Other useful items include a cutting board, a sharp knife, and a scrubbing brush.

Choosing a juicer

The most basic juicer is an electronic citrus press which juices only citrus fruits. For other fruit and vegetables you will need a juice extractor. With these machines you get what you pay for, so if you are serious about juicing it is worth investing in the best machine that you can afford.

There are two main mechanisms for juicers: centrifugal and masticating. In centrifugal juicers, the juice and pulp are separated by centrifugal force. Masticating juicers mash the fruit and push it through a mesh. These tend to be more expensive, but produce a larger quantity of juice.

key to recipe symbols

The quick-reference symbols beside each recipe indicate for which type of exercise the drink is most beneficial, and whether it is best enjoyed before, during, or after exercise. The activity symbols are listed directly below the time symbols for which they are appropriate. For example on page 31, Carrot and Kiwifruit juice is best before general fitness and during aerobic and low-intensity exercise.

 pre-exercise

 aerobic exercise *(see page 14)*

 extra-energy sports *(see page 15)*

 during exercise

 endurance activities *(see page 14)*

 muscular strength activities *(see page 17)*

 post-exercise

 low-intensity exercise *(see page 15)*

 general fitness *(see page 17)*

which drinks for which sport?

Which juices and smoothies are best before, during, and after each type of exercise.

table heading

sport category	pre-exercise	during exercise	post-exercise
aerobic exercise fitness classes/aerobic, running, swimming, cycling (leisure), power walking, social dancing	pages: 28, 32, 36, 38, 40, 42, 44, 52, 54, 56, 60, 92, 104, 110, 116	pages: 28, 30, 32, 38, 40, 42, 52, 56, 60, 68, 70, 74, 76, 80, 104, 106	pages: 32, 36, 42, 44, 46, 48, 54, 58, 60, 66, 72, 78, 82, 88, 90, 92, 94, 102, 104, 106, 108, 110, 112, 114, 116, 118, 122, 124
endurance activities long-distance running, triathlon, rowing, competition swimming, cross-country running, cycling (racing)	pages: 32, 42, 46, 48, 50, 52, 54, 56, 60, 64, 66, 82, 84, 110, 116, 120	pages: 32, 42, 52, 56, 60, 62, 68, 74, 76, 98, 100, 120	pages: 32, 42, 48, 54, 58, 60, 62, 64, 66, 72, 78, 82, 84, 88, 90, 94, 98, 100, 102, 108, 110, 112, 114, 116, 118, 120, 122, 124
low-intensity exercise walking, golf, cricket, scuba diving	pages: 28, 34, 36, 38, 40, 42, 44, 58, 60, 92, 94, 104, 116, 118, 120	pages: 28, 30, 38, 40, 42, 60, 86, 96, 98, 100, 104, 106, 120	pages: 36, 42, 44, 60, 86, 92, 96, 98, 100, 104, 106, 116, 120

sport category	pre-exercise	during exercise	post-exercise
extra-energy sports tennis, hockey, football, soccer, rugby, squash, circuit training, full-contact martial arts, water skiing (competition), basketball, netball	pages: 32, 42, 44, 52, 54, 56, 60, 64, 84, 110, 116	pages: 32, 42, 52, 56, 60, 62, 68, 70, 74, 76, 80, 100	pages: 32, 42, 44, 46, 48, 54, 58, 60, 62, 64, 66, 72, 78, 82, 84, 88, 90, 94, 100, 102, 108, 110, 112, 114, 116, 118, 122, 124
muscular strength activities	pages: 42, 110, 120	pages: 42, 76, 120	pages: 42, 46, 66, 82, 90, 94, 102, 108, 110, 112, 114, 118, 120, 122, 124
general fitness activities gym workouts, Pilates, yoga, body conditioning, water skiing, wakeboarding, sailing, roller skating, skateboarding, semi-contact martial arts, hiking, ice skating, playing with a Frisbee, housework, gardening, walking the dog	pages: 28, 30, 32, 34, 36, 38, 40, 42, 44, 52, 54, 56, 60, 64, 84, 92, 104, 110, 116, 120	pages: 26, 28, 32, 38, 40, 42, 52, 56, 60, 68, 70, 74, 76, 80, 86, 98, 100, 104, 106, 120	pages: 26, 32, 36, 42, 44, 46, 48, 54, 58, 60, 64, 84, 86, 88, 92, 94, 98, 100, 102, 104, 106, 108, 110, 112, 116, 118, 120, 122

carrot, apple, and ginger

A classic combination that is perfect during general fitness and lifestyle activities such as yoga and walking and after many other types of exercise. Ginger may help to alleviate symptoms of nausea, common among some athletes after strenuous competition.

2 carrots, about 7 oz in total
1 tart-flavored apple, such as
  Granny Smith
½ inch piece fresh ginger root

Scrub the carrots and wash the apple. Cut the carrots, apple, and ginger into even-size pieces and juice. Pour into a glass and add a couple of ice cubes. **Makes 1 cup; Serves 1**

Nutrition Notes

This juice is an excellent source of vitamins A, C, B1, B6, and potassium. In addition to being a natural remedy for travel sickness and morning sickness, ginger is also believed to aid digestion and help the body fight off colds.

Per serving

calories: 127
fat: 0.9 g
carbohydrate: 29 g
iron: 0.9 mg
calcium: 59 mg

watercress and pear

This juice is rich in several important nutrients and has a low glycemic index. It is ideal for topping up fluid stores before and during many sports activities, such as cycling and gym workouts, or before low-intensity sports, such as scuba diving. It can also be a useful alternative for those runners who find more concentrated fluids difficult to drink during exercise.

1 cup watercress
3 ripe pears

Wash the watercress well. Slice the pears into even-size pieces. Feed the pears and watercress into the juicer in alternating batches. Pour into a glass and add a couple of ice cubes.
Makes 1 cup; Serves 1

Nutrition Notes

Rich in vitamin C, beta-carotene, and cancer-fighting phytochemicals, the health benefits of watercress have been acknowledged for many centuries. Hippocrates wrote about its medicinal values in 460 BC and built the world's first hospital next to a stream so he could grow fresh watercress for his patients. This juice is an excellent source of vitamins C, B6, and beta-carotene. It also provides useful amounts of calcium.

Per serving

calories: 70
fat: 0.3 g
carbohydrate: 8 g
iron: 1.2 mg
calcium: 85 mg

carrot and kiwifruit

A delicious combination—the sharpness of the kiwifruit helps to cut through the sweetness of the carrot juice. Carrots are a good source of beta-carotene, the plant form of vitamin A, which is crucial for good vision, especially at night. This juice is therefore ideal for athletes who train or compete in low-light conditions.

**2 carrots, about 7 oz
  in total
1 kiwifruit**

Scrub the carrots. Cut the carrots and kiwifruit into even-size pieces and juice. Pour into a glass and add a couple of ice cubes. Decorate with slices of kiwifruit, if desired. **Makes 1 cup; Serves 1**

Nutrition Notes

Kiwifruit are an excellent source of vitamin C. They also provide good amounts of potassium and soluble fiber. Carrot and kiwifruit juice is an excellent source of vitamins A, C, B1, and B6.

Per serving

calories: 99
fat: 1 g
carbohydrate: 22 g
iron: 0.8 mg
calcium: 65 mg

31

beet, apple, and carrot

As beet has such a strong flavor it is best diluted, making it a great isotonic drink pre-, during, or post-exercise. Vitamin C, folic acid, and iron are all essential nutrients for athletes, making this juice a good choice for exercisers.

2 small beets
1 carrot
2 apples
1¼ cups water

Scrub the beets and carrot. Wash the apples. Cut all the ingredients into even-size pieces and juice. Add the water, then pour into a glass, adding a couple of ice cubes. **Makes 2½ cups; Serves 2**

Nutrition Notes

Beet is high in oxalic acid and should be avoided by anyone with oxalate kidney stones. This juice is an excellent source of vitamins A, C, B1, B6, folic acid, potassium, and phosphorus and provides useful amounts of iron.

Per serving

calories: 165
fat: 0.6 g
carbohydrate: 39 g
iron: 1.5 mg
calcium: 53 mg

celery, apple, and alfalfa

Although it provides good amounts of vitamins A, C, and K, alfalfa is rather bitter on its own and needs to be combined, as here, with sweeter flavors. This juice is perfect pre-exercise, especially before general fitness activities such as gardening. Because it contains a good amount of folic acid, it is particularly beneficial to female athletes.

3 celery sticks
2 tart-flavored apples, such as
  Granny Smith
1 cup alfalfa

Wash the celery and apples and cut into even-size pieces. Rinse the alfalfa. Feed all the ingredients into a juicer in alternating batches. Pour into a glass, add a couple of ice cubes, and drink immediately.
Makes 1 cup; Serves 1

Nutrition Notes

This juice is an excellent source of vitamin C, B6, and potassium and provides useful amounts of B1 and folic acid. Alfalfa, along with all other sprouted beans and seeds, is rich in vitamins B and C.

Per serving

calories: 106
fat: 0.6 g
carbohydrate: 24 g
iron: 0.8 mg
calcium: 53 mg

carrot, orange, and apple

A delicious combination of flavors, this juice is a good source of vitamins and fiber. Apples contain pectin, a type of soluble fiber that can help reduce high blood cholesterol levels. This is a good choice for vegetarian athletes as the vitamin C from the oranges helps the body absorb iron, something that non-meat eaters often lack.

2 carrots, about 7 oz in total
1 orange
1 tart-flavored apple, such as
  Granny Smith

Scrub the carrots. Peel the orange and divide into segments. Cut the carrots and apple into even-size pieces. Juice all the fruit, pour into a glass, then add a couple of ice cubes. **Makes 1 cup; Serves 1**

Nutrition Notes

Carrots are one of the richest sources of the antioxidant beta-carotene. This juice is an excellent source of vitamins C, B1, and B6, as well as folic acid and potassium. It provides useful amounts of calcium.

Per serving

calories: 160
fat: 0.8 g
carbohydrate: 38 g
iron: 0.8 mg
calcium: 110 mg

celery, tomato, and red sweet pepper

Ideal before general fitness activities, such as body-conditioning classes, this juice is an excellent source of vitamin C, which is involved in many of the body's metabolic processes, including those that are crucial for good functioning of the aerobic system. In addition, the vitamin C will aid the absorption of iron which is great for all athletes, particularly vegetarian athletes.

4 celery sticks
3 ripe tomatoes
½ red sweet pepper
½ red chili, seeded (optional)
1 clove garlic, crushed (optional)

Cut the vegetables into even-size pieces and juice. Pour into a glass, stir in the chili and crushed garlic, if using, and add a couple of ice cubes, if desired. **Makes 1¼ cups; Serves 1**

Nutrition Notes

Weight for weight, red sweet peppers contain over twice as much vitamin C as oranges. This juice is an excellent source of vitamins A, C, B1, B2, B6, folic acid, potassium, and phosphorus and provides useful amounts of iron and calcium.

Per serving

calories: 83
fat: 1.4 g
carbohydrate: 15 g
iron: 2.2 mg
calcium: 76 mg

celery, tomato, lemon, and parsley

This vibrant, fresh-tasting juice is packed full of nutrients. It provides 15 percent of our daily requirement of calcium, making it a good choice for all exercisers. For women athletes who may be prone to osteoporosis (brittle bone disease) it is a good drink to opt for before exercise. This juice is also an excellent source of iron, which is essential for athletes to prevent fatigue and anemia.

2 celery sticks
4 tomatoes
large handful of parsley
zest and juice of ½ lemon

Wash the celery, tomatoes, and parsley. Feed into the juicer in alternating batches, along with the lemon juice and zest. Pour the juice into a glass and add a couple of ice cubes. **1¼ cups; Serves 1**

Nutrition Notes

Eaten in reasonable quantities, parsley can provide useful amounts of vitamin C, iron, calcium, and potassium. Overall this juice is an excellent source of vitamins A, C, B1, B6, niacin, folic acid, iron, potassium, phosphorus, and magnesium and it also provides useful amounts of calcium.

Per serving

calories: 82
fat: 1.6 g
carbohydrate: 14 g
iron: 4 mg
calcium: 104 mg

41

carrot and pink grapefruit

Pink grapefruit are a good source of folic acid, essential to athletes as a deficiency could impair aerobic performance. They also contain lycopene, an antioxidant that protects the body against some cancers and lowers the risk of heart disease. This juice is isotonic, ideal for drinking pre-, during, and post-exercise. Pink grapefruit are sweeter than the yellow variety, making this drink more palatable.

2 carrots
2 apples
1 pink grapefruit
1¾ cups water

Scrub the carrots and wash the apples. Peel the grapefruit and divide into segments. Juice the carrots, apple, and grapefruit then add the water. Pour the juice into a glass and add a couple of ice cubes. Decorate with apple slices, if desired. **Makes 3 cups; Serves 2**

Nutrition Notes

Pink grapefruit is a good source of the phytochemical lycopene. This juice is an excellent source of vitamins A, C, B1, B6, folic acid, and potassium and provides useful amounts of calcium—essential for healthy bones.

Per serving

calories: 210
fat: 1 g
carbohydrate: 50 g
iron: 1 mg
calcium: 95 mg

spinach, carrot, and tomato

Spinach is a useful source of iron. It also contains good amounts of vitamins C, E, B1, and B6, and folic acid. Vitamin B1 is particularly important to the sports person as it is involved in the conversion of carbohydrates into energy and is used for the normal functioning of nerves and muscle tissue. Vitamin E is also useful for athletes, as it offers optimal immune responses to exercise-induced injury.

large handful of baby spinach
2 carrots, about 7 oz in total
4 tomatoes
½ red sweet pepper

Wash and drain the spinach. Scrub the carrots and wash the tomatoes and pepper. Juice the vegetables in alternating batches. Pour the juice into a glass and add a couple of ice cubes. **Makes 1¼ cups; Serves 1**

Nutrition Notes

This juice is an excellent source of vitamins A, C, B1, B6, niacin, folic acid, iron, calcium, potassium, magnesium, and phosphorus and provides useful amounts of vitamin E.

Per serving

calories: 175
fat: 2.5 g
carbohydrate: 34 g
iron: 3.8 mg
calcium: 169 mg

apple, mango, and passion fruit

To counteract the sweetness of the mango it's best to use a slightly tart variety of apple. High in carbohydrate, this juice is a great energy giver, so it is most suitable after exercise. It can also be a good choice before an endurance event, when high levels of energy are required and when an athlete may find solid food hard to tolerate.

3 apples, preferably red ones
1 mango
2 passion fruit

Wash the apples, peel the mango and remove the pit. Cut the mango and apples into even-size pieces. Slice the passion fruit in half, scoop out the flesh, and discard the seeds. Juice all the ingredients. Pour the juice into a glass and add a couple of ice cubes.
Makes 1¼ cups; Serves 1

Nutrition Notes

This juice is an excellent source of vitamins A and C, potassium, magnesium, and phosphorus and provides useful amounts of iron.

Per serving

calories: 240
fat: 0.7 g
carbohydrate: 58 g
iron: 1.7 mg
calcium: 33 mg

47

pear and pineapple

A good drink to choose before or after most activities including extra-energy sports, such as circuit training and basketball. Pineapples contain an enzyme, bromelain, that breaks down protein. This juice is rich in B vitamins. These help release energy from carbohydrate—essential for all athletes, especially those who practice aerobic, endurance, or extra-energy sports.

2 pears
¼ pineapple, about 7½ oz
  flesh, once skin and core
  have been removed
½ lime

Wash the pears. Remove the skin and hard central core from the pineapple. Scrub the lime. Chop the fruit into even-size pieces and juice it. Pour into a glass and add a couple of ice cubes, if desired.
Makes 1¼ cups; Serves 1

Nutrition Notes

This juice is an excellent source of vitamins C, B1, B6, calcium, and copper.

Per serving

calories: 212
fat: 0.8 g
carbohydrate: 53 g
iron: 1 mg
calcium: 74 mg

49

pear, kiwifruit, and lime

Weight for weight, kiwifruit, contain more vitamin C than oranges. Athletes often suffer muscle damage during training and, even with precautions, often seem to attract bangs, knocks and other injuries. Ensuring that there is enough vitamin C in your diet helps protect against muscle damage, and leads to a reduction in muscle soreness and improved general healing. Vitamin C may also help to increase oxygen uptake and aerobic energy production.

2 ripe pears
3 kiwifruit
½ lime

Wash the pears, peel the kiwifruit and scrub the lime. Slice the fruit into even-sized pieces, then juice. Pour into a glass, add a couple of ice cubes, and decorate with slices of pear, if desired.
Makes 1¼ cups; Serves 1

Nutrition Notes

This juice is an excellent source of vitamins C and B6, copper, magnesium, and phosphorus and provides useful amounts of calcium.

Per serving

calories: 210
fat: 1.2 g
carbohydrate: 49 g
iron: 1.3 mg
calcium: 78 mg

strawberry, red currant, and orange

This juice provides good amounts of calcium and iron, which make it a good choice before or during most types of exercise. Calcium is important for good bone health, while the iron helps to prevent fatigue and optimizes general performance. A good iron intake is especially important for those who take part in contact sports, and for female athletes, vegetarian and vegan athletes, and athletes who are pregnant.

1½ cups strawberries
1⅓ cups red currants
1 orange
1 cup water
1 teaspoon clear honey (optional)

Wash and hull the strawberries and red currants. Peel the orange and divide it into segments. Juice the fruit, then add the water. Pour into a glass, stir in the honey, if using, and add a couple of ice cubes, if desired. **Makes 2 cups; Serves 2**

Nutrition Notes

This juice is an excellent source of vitamins C, B1, B2, niacin, B6, folic acid, copper, potassium, calcium, magnesium, and phosphorus and provides useful amounts of iron. It is a great, all-round choice for sports activities.

Per serving

calories: 150
fat: 0.4 g
carbohydrate: 33 g
iron: 2.8 mg
calcium: 161 mg

apple and plum

If you choose plums that are ripe but not over-ripe, you will find it easier to remove the pits before juicing. Potassium levels are quite high in this juice. Potassium is a vital mineral for muscle and nerve function and helps to regulate blood pressure. It is useful for athletes before and after exercise, particularly when the appetite is reduced but it is necessary for carbohydrate and fluid to be replaced.

5 ripe dessert plums
3 red apples

Wash the fruit. Slice the plums into quarters and remove the pits. Cut the apples into even-size pieces. Juice the fruit and serve in a glass over a couple of ice cubes. **Makes 1¼ cups; Serves 1**

Nutrition Notes

Apples are a good source of pectin, a type of soluble fiber that can help to reduce high blood cholesterol levels. Because pectin is water-soluble apple juice retains reasonable amounts of pectin. This juice is an excellent source of vitamins A, C, B6, niacin, copper, and potassium.

Per serving

calories: 210
fat: 0.5 g
carbohydrate: 52 g
iron: 1 mg
calcium: 36 mg

apple and blackberry

Apple and blackberry is a classic combination. Blackberries can be tart so it is best to choose a sweeter variety of apple, such as Braeburn, Pink Lady, Cox's Orange Pippin, or Golden Delicious. Blackberries are rich in the antioxidant vitamins C and E and this juice provides an excellent amount of vitamin E.

3 apples
1 cup blackberries
1¼ cups water

Wash the fruit. Slice the apples into even-size pieces. Juice the fruit then stir in the water. Pour into a glass and add a couple of ice cubes.
Makes 2½ *cups*; Serves 2

Nutrition Notes

This juice is an excellent source of vitamins C, E, B6, copper, magnesium, and phosphorus and provides useful amounts of calcium, which is so important for bone health in athletes.

Per serving

calories: 179
fat: 0.6 g
carbohydrate: 43 g
iron: 1.3 mg
calcium: 74 mg

melon, pineapple, and apple

Melon and pineapple are both quite sweet so it's best to use a tart variety of apple to counterbalance the flavors. High in water content, melons add a refreshing flavor to juices, making them ideal before low-intensity activities. This juice has quite a high carbohydrate content, so it is good for providing fuel for sports activity.

½ *Galia melon, about 13 oz*
¼ *pineapple, about 7½ oz flesh, once skin and core have been removed*
1 green apple

Remove the skin and seeds from the melon. Remove the skin and hard central core from the pineapple. Wash the apple. Chop the fruit into even-size pieces and juice. Pour into a glass and add a couple of ice cubes.
Makes 1¼ cups; Serves 1

Nutrition Notes

Pineapples contain an enzyme called bromelain that breaks down protein. Some studies suggest bromelain may help treat blood clots that can cause thrombosis. This juice is an excellent source of vitamins C, B1, B2, B6, copper, potassium, magnesium, and phosphorus and provides useful amounts of calcium.

Per serving

calories: 235
fat: 1 g
carbohydrate: 57 g
iron: 1.3 mg
calcium: 97 mg

59

watermelon
and raspberry

A refreshing juice that can be drunk at almost any time by most athletes. Watermelons are classed as having a high glycemic index, so juices containing watermelon are good to drink during or after exercise to aid fast muscle refueling, particularly when fluid replacement is a priority.

¼ **watermelon, about**
10 oz flesh
1 cup raspberries

Remove the skin and seeds from the watermelon and chop the flesh into even-size pieces. Juice the watermelon and raspberries, pour into a large glass, and add a couple of ice cubes.
Makes 1½ cups; Serves 1

Nutrition Notes

This juice is an excellent source of vitamins A, C, B1, folic acid, magnesium, and phosphorus.

Per serving

calories: 125
fat: 1.3 g
carbohydrate: 27 g
iron: 1.8 mg
calcium: 52 mg

melon and grape

This isotonic juice is particularly suitable during extra-energy and endurance activities when a thirst-quenching drink is required. Grapes are a good source of potassium and make the perfect energy snack after these types of exercise.

½ *Galia melon, about 10 oz*
1 cup seedless green grapes
1¼ cups water

Remove the skin and the seeds from the melon and chop the flesh into even-size pieces. Wash the grapes. Juice the fruit then add the water. Pour the juice into a glass and add a couple of ice cubes, if desired. **Makes 2½ cups; Serves 2**

Nutrition Notes

This juice is an excellent source of vitamins C, B1, B6, copper, magnesium, and phosphorus.

Per serving

calories: 180
fat: 0.5 g
carbohydrate: 44 g
iron: 1 mg
calcium: 62 mg

watermelon
and orange

This is the perfect juice to drink before an endurance or extra-energy activity, or after general fitness sports. As well as copious amounts of vitamin C, it provides potassium, which is vital for muscle and nerve function during exercise. Watermelons have a high glycemic index, making them ideal after exercise when fluid requirements are high and refueling muscle stores is paramount.

¼ watermelon, about 10 oz
    flesh
2 oranges

Remove the skin and seeds from the watermelon and chop the flesh into even-size pieces. Peel the oranges and divide the flesh into segments. Juice the fruit, pour it into a glass, and add a couple of ice cubes. Decorate with slices of orange, if desired.
Makes 1¼ cups; Serves 1

Nutrition Notes

This juice is an excellent source of vitamins C and B6, folic acid, calcium, copper, and potassium, which help provide energy and improve muscle and nerve function.

Per serving

calories: 200
fat: 1 g
carbohydrate: 47 g
iron: 1.2 mg
calcium: 162 mg

melon, kiwifruit, and grape

This is a great juice to drink before an endurance event, when you want to fill your body with as many nutrients as possible, without drinking anything too heavy. It provides good amounts of calcium and carbohydrate. In addition, the large amount of vitamin C in kiwifruit protects against muscle damage, reduces muscle soreness, and accelerates healing after injury.

12 oz honeydew melon
2 kiwifruit
¾ cup seedless green grapes

Remove the skin and seeds from the melon. Peel the kiwifruit. Chop the melon and kiwifruits into even-size pieces. Juice all the fruit, pour into a glass, and add a couple of ice cubes.
Makes 1¼ cups; Serves 1

Nutrition Notes

This juice is an excellent source of vitamins C, B6, and B1, as well as copper, potassium, magnesium, and phosphorus and also provides useful amounts of calcium, essential for healthy bones and bone strength, as well as protecting against osteoporosis.

Per serving

calories: 232
fat: 1 g
carbohydrate: 55 g
iron: 1.2 mg
calcium: 78 mg

orange and raspberry

This is an excellent isotonic drink containing plenty of calcium, which is great for drinking during endurance, extra-energy, or general fitness activity, as it gives a good boost of vitamin C, plus potassium and folate. Folate is essential for women of child-bearing age because it helps protect against birth defects.

2 large oranges
1½ cups raspberries
1 cup water

Peel the oranges and divide the flesh into segments. Wash the raspberries. Juice the fruit then add the water. Pour into a glass and add a couple of ice cubes. **Makes 2 cups; Serves 2**

Nutrition Notes

This juice is an excellent source of vitamins C, B6, B1, folate, zinc, copper, calcium, and potassium and provides useful amounts of iron.

Per serving

calories: 155
fat: 0.8 g
carbohydrate: 34 g
iron: 1.5 mg
calcium: 185 mg

orange and apricot

Fresh apricots have a short season so it's important to make the most of them when they are available. They produce a deliciously sweet, luxurious-tasting juice. If you can't get fresh apricots try peaches or nectarines. This juice is good during exercise as it contains plenty of calcium and iron, as well as beta-carotene, the plant form of vitamin A. Beta-carotene is essential for good vision; it also helps to fight damage caused by free radicals and can therefore protect against some cancers.

10 oz apricots
1 large orange
1¼ cups water

Wash the apricots and remove the pits. Peel the orange and divide the flesh into segments. Juice the fruit then add the water. Pour into a glass and add ice cubes, if desired. **Makes 2½ cups; Serves 2**

Nutrition Notes

This juice is an excellent source of vitamins C, A, B6, folic acid, magnesium, phosphorus, copper, and potassium and provides useful amounts of calcium and iron, making it a good, all-round choice for athletes.

Per serving

calories: 150
fat: 0.5 g
carbohydrate: 34 g
iron: 1.6 mg
calcium: 116 mg

orange, cranberry, and mango

Oranges, cranberries, and mangoes are packed with the antioxidant vitamin C. Women with urinary tract infections will find cranberries a good natural treatment. When fresh cranberries are not in season, use frozen cranberries instead but defrost them first.

½ cup cranberries
1 mango
1 orange
½ cup water
1 teaspoon clear honey

Wash the cranberries. Peel the mango and remove the pit. Peel the orange and divide the flesh into segments. Juice the fruit, pour into a glass, and stir in the water and honey. Add a couple of ice cubes and drink immediately. Decorate with cranberries, if desired. **Makes 1¾ cups; Serves 1**

Nutrition Notes

This juice is an excellent source of vitamins A and C and provides useful amounts of B1, B6, copper, potassium, calcium, and iron. It is a good choice before exercise as it helps to offset injury problems.

Per serving

calories: 183
fat: 0.6 g
carbohydrate: 44 g
iron: 2.1 mg
calcium: 104 mg

pink grapefruit
and pineapple

This is a delicious thirst-quencher in which the sweetness of the pineapple perfectly complements the more tart flavor of the pink grapefruit. It is an ideal drink during almost every type of exercise, but remember that the phytochemicals in grapefruit juice can interfere with the breakdown of certain drugs such as those used to treat high blood pressure, heart problems, and asthma, increasing the risk of side effects.

1 pink grapefruit
¼ pineapple, about 7½ oz flesh, once skin and core have been removed
1¼ cups water

Peel the grapefruit and divide the flesh into segments. Remove the skin and hard central core from the pineapple and slice the flesh into even-size pieces. Juice the fruit then add the water. Pour into a glass and add a couple of ice cubes. **Makes 2½ cups; Serves 2**

Nutrition Notes

This juice is an excellent source of vitamins C and B6, folic acid, copper, and potassium, as well as providing useful amounts of calcium.

Per serving

calories: 140
fat: 0.6 g
carbohydrate: 33 g
iron: 0.6 mg
calcium: 77 mg

strawberry and kiwifruit

Packed with vitamin C, this juice is great during exercise, as vitamin C is thought to increase oxygen uptake and aerobic energy production. Kiwifruit are also a good source of potassium, which is needed for nerve and muscle function.

1 cup strawberries
2 kiwifruit

Wash and hull the strawberries. Peel the kiwifruit and slice them into even-size pieces. Juice the fruit, pour it into a glass then add a couple of ice cubes, if desired. **Makes 1¼ cups; Serves 1**

Nutrition Notes

This juice is an excellent source of vitamin C, potassium, copper, magnesium, and phosphorus, making it a good choice during exercise, when the body needs to maintain high levels of nutrients for performance.

Per serving

calories: 100
fat: 0.8 g
carbohydrate: 22 g
iron: 1 mg
calcium: 54 mg

orange, apple, and pear

This juice is especially good after an endurance event such as a cycle race as it contains large amounts of carbohydrate, essential for refueling energy stores lost during competition. It is also a good source of calcium. Many athletes cannot face solid food after grueling exercise, so a juice like this one is ideal. The addition of honey gives an extra energy boost, which may be very welcome.

2 oranges
1 red apple
1 pear
1 teaspoon clear honey
  (optional)

Peel the oranges and divide the flesh into segments. Wash the apple and pear and chop them into even-size pieces. Juice the fruit and pour it into a glass. Stir in the honey, if using, and add a couple of ice cubes. **Makes 1½ cups; Serves 1**

Nutrition Notes

This juice is an excellent source of vitamins C, B1, B2, B6, folic acid, calcium, copper, potassium, magnesium, and phosphorus, making it a great way for athletes to replenish energy and nutrient stores after an endurance event.

Per serving

calories: 218
fat: 0.6 g
carbohydrate: 52 g
iron: 0.7 mg
calcium: 162 mg

strawberry, peach, and apple

This juice provides useful amounts of iron, which is an important mineral for all athletes, particularly women, as it aids the transport of oxygen around the body. A deficiency in iron can adversely affect performance, both in training and competition.

¾ cup strawberries
2 peaches
1 red apple
1¼ cups water

Wash and hull the strawberries. Wash the peaches and apple. Remove the pits from the peaches. Chop the fruit into even-size chunks and juice it. Add the water, then pour the juice into a glass and add a couple of ice cubes, if desired.
Makes 2½ cups; Serves 2

Nutrition Notes

This juice is an excellent source of vitamin C, copper, potassium, magnesium, and phosphorus. It also contains useful amounts of iron.

Per serving

calories: 153
fat: 0.4 g
carbohydrate: 36 g
iron: 1.5 mg
calcium: 39 mg

grape and kiwifruit

Kiwifruit are an excellent source of vitamin C. When choosing them select ones that are firm to the touch but not rock hard. This juice is a good choice before an endurance event such as rowing as it contains large amounts of carbohydrate for energy release, plus a hefty amount of vitamin C, to protect against muscle soreness and injury. Vitamin C may also help to increase oxygen uptake and aerobic energy production.

2 kiwifruit
1½ cups seedless green grapes

Peel the kiwifruit, chop them into even-size pieces, and juice them with the grapes. Pour the juice into a glass and add a couple of ice cubes. Decorate with grapes, if desired. **Makes 1¼ cups; Serves 1**

Nutrition Notes

This juice is an excellent source of vitamins C, B1, B6, copper, potassium, magnesium, and phosphorus and also provides useful amounts of calcium.

Per serving

calories: 240
fat: 0.9 g
carbohydrate: 59 g
iron: 1.4 mg
calcium: 69 mg

grape and plum

Choose this juice before any endurance, extra-energy, or general fitness activity. It is a good source of potassium, vitamin E, and iron. Potassium enhances muscle and nerve function, while vitamin E is a powerful antioxidant, protecting against free radical damage and so protecting against some cancers. Iron prevents fatigue and anemia and can positively affect performance. Interestingly, red grapes contain more antioxidant than green ones.

1 cup seedless red grapes
5 plums, about 10 oz

Wash the grapes and plums. Remove the pits from the plums then cut the flesh into even-size pieces. Juice the fruit, pour it into a glass, and add a couple of ice cubes. Decorate with slices of plum, if desired. **Makes 1¼ cups; Serves 1**

Nutrition Notes

This juice is an excellent source of vitamins A, C, B1, niacin, B6, copper, and potassium and also provides useful amounts of iron.

Per serving

calories: 190
fat: 0.5 g
carbohydrate: 48 g
iron: 1.6 mg
calcium: 56 mg

apricot smoothie

This smoothie is an excellent source of calcium, providing almost one-third of the daily requirement. Calcium is essential for helping to build and maintain good bone health, and is also involved in nerve transmission, blood clotting, and muscle function. Canned apricots in natural juice are a handy standby to have in your pantry and provide an extra source of carbohydrate.

7 oz can apricots in natural juice, drained
⅔ cup apricot yogurt
⅔ cup ice-cold lowfat milk

Place the apricots, yogurt, and milk in a food processor or blender and process until smooth. Add a couple of ice cubes, pour into a glass, decorate with slices of apricot, if desired, and drink immediately. **Makes 1¾ cups; Serves 1**

Nutrition Notes

This smoothie is an excellent source of vitamins A, C, B1, B2, B6, and B12, as well as calcium, potassium, zinc, magnesium, and phosphorus.

Per serving

calories: 140
fat: 2 g
carbohydrate: 24 g
protein: 7 g
iron: 0.46 mg
calcium: 221 mg

banana and peanut butter smoothie

Peanut butter may sound an unusual ingredient in a smoothie, but in fact it combines wonderfully well with bananas to make a rich, satisfying drink. Peanuts contain resveratrol, plant sterols, and other phytochemicals which, according to research, have cardio-protective and cancer-inhibiting properties. This high-calcium drink is a great pick-me-up after exercise.

1 ripe banana
1¼ cups lowfat milk
1 tablespoon smooth peanut butter or 2 teaspoons tahini paste

Peel and slice the banana, put it in a freezer container and freeze for at least 2 hours or overnight. Put the banana, milk, and peanut butter or tahini paste in a food processor or blender and process until smooth. Serve immediately. **Makes 1¾ cups; Serves 1**

Nutrition Notes

Tahini is a delicious paste made from crushed sesame seeds. Weight for weight, sesame seeds contain ten times more calcium than milk. This smoothie is an excellent source of vitamins C, B1, B2, B6, B12, folic acid, niacin, calcium, copper, potassium, zinc, magnesium, and phosphorus.

Per serving

calories: 326
fat: 13 g
carbohydrate: 40 g
protein: 14 g
iron: 0.8 mg
calcium: 372 mg

banana, strawberry, and orange smoothie

It is important that exercisers start to refuel their muscle glycogen as soon as possible after exercise and so this high-carbohydrate, low-fat smoothie is a great choice. Bananas are high in potassium, a vital mineral for muscle and nerve function, which also helps to regulate blood pressure.

1 small ripe banana
½ cup strawberries
1 cup orange juice

Peel and slice the banana. Wash, hull and roughly chop the strawberries. Place the fruit into a freezer container and freeze for at least 2 hours or overnight. Place the frozen fruit and the orange juice in a food processor or blender and process until thick. Decorate with strawberries, if desired, and serve immediately. **Makes 1¾ cups; Serves 1**

Nutrition Notes

This smoothie is an excellent source of vitamins C, B1, B6, folic acid, potassium, magnesium, and phosphorus.

Per serving

calories: 200
fat: 0.4 g
carbohydrate: 48 g
protein: 4 g
iron: 1.3 mg
calcium: 48 mg

avocado and banana smoothie

This smoothie is suitable before carrying out low-intensity and general fitness activities. Bananas provide carbohydrate and energy, while avocados supply the body with healthy unsaturated fats. Drinking this will help to fuel the body and maintain good energy levels. Using skim milk helps keep down the overall fat content.

1 small ripe avocado
1 small ripe banana
1 cup skim milk

Peel the avocado, remove the pit and roughly chop the flesh. Peel and slice the banana. Place the avocado, banana, and milk in a food processor or blender and process until smooth. Pour into a glass, add a couple of ice cubes, and drink immediately.
Makes 1¾ cups; Serves 1

Nutrition Notes

Most of the fat in avocados is monounsaturated, which helps lower levels of the "bad" cholesterol (or low-density lipoproteins) while raising levels of the "good" cholesterol (or high-density lipoproteins). Just one avocado provides around half the recommended daily intake of vitamin B6. This smoothie is an excellent source of vitamins C, E, B1, B2, B6, and B12, as well as folic acid, calcium, potassium, copper, zinc, magnesium, and phosphorus.

Per serving

calories: 270
fat: 20 g
carbohydrate: 37 g
protein: 11 g
iron: 0.85 mg
calcium: 317 mg

mango, pineapple, and lime smoothie

This smoothie is a good choice after most activities. It contains the 50 g (2 oz) carbohydrate commonly recommended to help refuel glycogen stores in the muscles after exercise—ideally it should be drunk within 1–2 hours of finishing the activity. It is also rich in B vitamins, which help the body to optimize energy production and performance.

1 ripe mango
1¼ cups pineapple juice
zest and juice of ½ lime

Peel the mango, remove the pit, roughly chop the flesh and put it in a freezer container. Freeze for at least 2 hours or overnight. Place the frozen mango in a food processor or blender with the pineapple juice and lime zest and juice and process until thick. Decorate with lime wedges, if desired, and serve immediately. **Makes 1¾ cups; Serves 1**

Nutrition Notes

This smoothie is an excellent source of vitamins A, C, B1, B2, B6, copper, potassium, magnesium, and phosphorus and provides useful amounts of iron.

Per serving

calories: 210
fat: 0.6 g
carbohydrate: 53 g
protein: 2 g
iron: 1.6 mg
calcium: 42 mg

banana and almond smoothie

The combination of bananas, ground almonds, and soy milk makes this a highly nutritious drink. Bananas are a very popular source of carbohydrate among endurance athletes, and they can be eaten before, during, or after exercise, making them hugely versatile. It is best to use very ripe bananas.

2 very ripe bananas
1¾ cups soya milk
⅓ cup ground almonds
pinch of ground cinnamon
a little honey (optional)

Peel and slice the bananas, put them into a freezer container and freeze for at least 2 hours. Place the frozen bananas, soy milk, ground almonds, and cinnamon in a food processor or blender, add the honey, if using, and process until thick and frothy. Pour into glasses and serve with ice cubes and slivered almonds. **Makes 2½ cups; Serves 2**

Nutrition Notes

Almonds are an excellent source of vitamin E as well as the minerals calcium, magnesium, phosphorus, and copper. They also help to increase the protein content of this drink, which is an excellent source of vitamins C, E, B1, B2, B6, niacin, folic acid, copper, potassium, zinc, magnesium, and phosphorus and provides useful amounts of calcium.

Per serving

calories: 330
fat: 15 g
carbohydrate: 34 g
protein: 12 g
iron: 1.8 mg
calcium: 85 mg

summer berry smoothie

Summer berries are packed with vitamin C and B vitamins. They have a deep color and rich flavor and so are ideal for making smoothies. Nutritionally, frozen fruit is every bit as good as fresh, and it is available all year round. Soy milk is a good alternative to cows' milk for those who are lactose-intolerant, but look for a calcium-enriched brand for maximum nutrition. This smoothie is isotonic and so may be consumed during sport, particularly low-intensity and low-impact exercises.

1 cup frozen mixed summer
berries
1¼ cups vanilla-flavored soy milk
1 teaspoon clear honey (optional)

Place the berries, soy milk, and honey, if using, in a food processor or blender and process until thick. Serve immediately decorated with berries, if desired. **Makes 1¾ cups; Serves 1**

Nutrition Notes

This drink is an excellent source of vitamins C, B1, B2, B6, folic acid, copper, potassium, zinc, magnesium, and phosphorus and provides useful amounts of calcium and iron. It is a good, all-round smoothie for general fitness activities.

Per serving

calories: 160
fat: 6 g
carbohydrate: 18 g
protein: 10 g
iron: 2.2 mg
calcium: 80 mg

peach and orange smoothie

This delicious smoothie is ideal during endurance events or after most activities, particularly when fluid replacement is a priority. Exercise, with adequate calcium intake, helps prevent bone loss and the yogurt provides a good source of calcium.

13 oz can peaches in natural juice, drained
⅔ cup peach or apricot yogurt
¾ cup orange juice
a little honey (optional)

Place the peaches in a food processor or blender with the yogurt, orange juice, and honey, if using, and process until smooth. Add a couple of ice cubes, if desired, and drink immediately.
Makes 2 cups; Serves 2

Nutrition Notes

This smoothie is an excellent source of vitamins C, B1, B2, B6, folic acid, calcium, potassium, and phosphorus, making it an ideal drink after almost any exercise.

Per serving

calories: 170
fat: 2 g
carbohydrate: 34 g
protein: 6 g
iron: 1.2 mg
calcium: 170 mg

prune, apple, and cinnamon smoothie

This smoothie is rich in carbohydrate, so it is an excellent way to replenish muscle and liver glycogen after exercise. This is particularly helpful in extra-energy, endurance and muscular strength activities where muscle glycogen stores are likely to be depleted. Prunes are also a useful source of iron. It might be wise to avoid drinking this juice before exercise owing to the laxative qualities of prunes.

⅓ cup ready-to-eat prunes
pinch of ground cinnamon
1½ cups apple juice
3 tablespoons whole milk yogurt

Roughly chop the prunes into small pieces. Put the prunes and cinnamon in a large bowl. Pour over the apple juice, cover and allow to stand overnight. Place the prunes, apple juice, and yogurt in a food processor or blender and process until smooth. Pour into a glass, add ice cubes, sprinkle with cinnamon, and drink immediately. **Makes 1¾ cups; Serves 1**

Nutrition Notes

This smoothie is an excellent source of vitamins C, B2, B6, potassium, magnesium, and phosphorus and provides useful amounts of calcium and iron.

Per serving

calories: 270
fat: 5 g
carbohydrate: 56 g
protein: 5 g
iron: 2 mg
calcium: 112 mg

rhubarb and custard smoothie

Rhubarb is a great source of potassium and also contains vitamin C and manganese. However, it should form only a small part of an athlete's diet as it also contains oxalic acid, which can inhibit the absorption of calcium and iron. The custard and milk ensure that this smoothie is calcium-rich, which will offset the negative effect of oxalic acid.

5 oz can rhubarb
5 oz container ready-made custard
½ cup ice-cold lowfat milk
1 teaspoon confectioners' sugar (optional)

Drain the rhubarb then put it into a food processor or blender with the custard, milk, and confectioners' sugar, if using, and process until smooth. Pour into a glass, add a couple of ice cubes, if desired, and serve immediately.
Makes 1¾ cups; Serves 1

Nutrition Notes

This smoothie is an excellent source of B2, B12, calcium, and phosphorus. Lowfat milk contains as much calcium as whole milk, but has fewer calories, so it is useful for those who are watching their weight.

Per serving

calories: 135
fat: 4 g
carbohydrate: 21 g
protein: 5 g
iron: 0.7 mg
calcium: 185 mg

cucumber
and mint lassi

Refreshing and summery, this smoothie is based on the Indian drink lassi. It contains a large amount of calcium, essential for bone health, while the cucumber's high water content makes it a good choice for quenching the thirst after activity. As it is isotonic it is easily absorbed and ideal when glycogen refueling is not the priority.

½ *cucumber, 7 oz*
1 cup plain bio yogurt
handful of chopped mint
¼ *teaspoon salt (optional)*

Slice the cucumber in half lengthwise and, using a teaspoon, remove and discard the seeds. Roughly chop the flesh and place it in a food processor or blender with the yogurt, mint, and salt, if using, and process until smooth. Pour into a glass, add a couple of ice cubes, decorate with mint, if desired, and drink immediately. **Makes 1¼ cups; Serves 1**

Nutrition Notes

This smoothie is an excellent source of vitamins A, C, B1, B2, B6, B12, folic acid, potassium, zinc, magnesium, phosphorus, and calcium—it is good after most sports.

Per serving

calories: 220
fat: 8 g
carbohydrate: 22 g
protein: 15 g
iron: 0.8 mg
calcium: 536 mg

apricot and pineapple smoothie

Dried apricots have an increased concentration of beta-carotene, potassium, and iron, making them especially useful for athletes. Drunk after exercise, this smoothie helps to refuel the muscles and helps to boost energy levels that may have been depleted, particularly after endurance activities such as long-distance running.

⅓ cup ready-to-eat dried apricots
1½ cups pineapple juice

Roughly chop the apricots into small pieces and put them in a large bowl. Pour the pineapple juice over them, cover the bowl, and allow to stand overnight. Tip the contents of the bowl into a food processor or blender and process until smooth. Add a couple of ice cubes and drink immediately.
Makes 1½ cups; Serves 1

Nutrition Notes

Dried apricots are a useful source of calcium particularly for anyone on a dairy-free diet. Many brands of dried apricots are preserved using sulfur dioxide, which can trigger asthma attacks. To avoid this, check the packaging before you buy, or rinse the apricots well before eating them. This smoothie is an excellent source of vitamins C, B1 and B6, copper, potassium, magnesium, and phosphorus and provides useful amounts of calcium and iron.

Per serving

calories: 240
fat: 0.7 g
carbohydrate: 59 g
protein: 3.5 g
iron: 2.7 mg
calcium: 72 mg

blackberry and grape smoothie

Blackberries and purple grape juice contain antioxidants that are excellent for the general health of athletes and exercisers. In addition, purple grape juice is a good source of potassium, which is essential for optimum nerve, cell, and muscle function. Adding Quark gives this drink a creamy taste and texture and also boosts the calcium and protein content. If you cannot find Quark use plain bio yogurt instead.

¾ cup frozen blackberries
1¼ cups purple grape juice
3 tablespoons Quark
1 teaspoon clear honey (optional)

Put the blackberries, grape juice, and Quark in a food processor or blender, add the honey, if using, and process until thick. Decorate with a few blackberries and serve immediately.

Makes 1¾ cups; Serves 1

Nutrition Notes

Purple grape juice contains high levels of bioflavoids, antioxidants like those found in red wine, which can help protect against heart disease. Studies have shown that drinking one large glass of purple grape juice a day is as effective as drinking two glasses of red wine in preventing heart disease. This smoothie is an excellent source of vitamins C, B1, B2, B6, B12, folic acid, calcium, iron, magnesium, and phosphorus.

Per serving

calories: 200
fat: 0.6 g
carbohydrate: 42 g
protein: 9 g
iron: 3.5 mg
calcium: 162 mg

cranberry and mango smoothie

Containing high levels of carbohydrate for energy, and calcium for bone health and strength, this smoothie is ideal for many athletes. Cranberry juice is a natural way of fighting urinary tract infections, which can blight training and performance for female athletes in particular.

1 ripe mango
¾ cup cranberry juice
⅔ cup peach yogurt

Peel the mango, remove the pit and roughly chop the flesh. Place the flesh in a food processor or blender with the cranberry juice and yogurt and process until smooth. Pour into a glass, add a couple of ice cubes, decorate with slices of mango, if desired, and drink immediately.
Makes 1¾ cups; Serves 1

Nutrition Notes

This smoothie is an excellent source of vitamins A, C, B1, B2, B6, and B12, folic acid, calcium, zinc, potassium, magnesium, and phosphorus and also provides useful amounts of iron.

Per serving

calories: 280
fat: 5 g
carbohydrate: 52 g
protein: 10 g
iron: 1.4 mg
calcium: 332 mg

orange, mango, and strawberry smoothie

As it contains useful amounts of calcium, iron, and carbohydrate and has low fat levels, this smoothie is perfect after endurance events or for athletes who practice exercises such as weight-training. This is because it replaces energy and raises iron levels, while also helping to maintain bone health.

¾ cup strawberries
1 small ripe mango
1¼ cups orange juice

Wash and hull the strawberries, place them in a freezer container and freeze for 2 hours or overnight. Peel the mango, remove the pit, roughly chop the flesh and place in a food processor or blender with the strawberries and orange juice and process until thick. Decorate with slices of orange, if desired, and serve immediately.
Makes 1¾ cups; Serves 1

Nutrition Notes

This smoothie is an excellent source of vitamins A, C, B1, B2, B6, folic acid, copper, potassium, magnesium, and phosphorus and also provides useful amounts of calcium and iron.

Per serving

calories: 230

fat: 0.7 g

carbohydrate: 55 g

protein: 3.5 g

iron: 2.1 mg

calcium: 68 mg

tropical fruit smoothie

Versatility is the key to this smoothie. It is likely to be well absorbed, as it is isotonic, and provides a good source of carbohydrate to fuel activity and refuel afterwards. It is also a very good source of calcium, which is essential for bone health and strength. Bananas and mangoes also supply fiber, making this a filling and satisfying smoothie.

1 large banana
1 large ripe mango
⅔ cup plain bio yogurt
1¼ cups pineapple juice

Peel and slice the banana, then put it in a freezer container and freeze for at least 2 hours or overnight. Peel the mango, remove the pit and roughly chop the flesh. Place it in a food processor or blender with the frozen banana, yogurt, and pineapple juice. Process until smooth and serve immediately, decorated with pineapple cubes, if desired. **Makes 2½ cups; Serves 2**

Nutrition Notes

This smoothie is an excellent source of vitamins A, C, B1, B2, B6, folic acid, calcium, potassium, copper, magnesium, and phosphorus. Adding yogurt to a smoothie is an effective way to increase its calcium content.

Per serving

calories: 230
fat: 2.8 g
carbohydrate: 48 g
protein: 6 g
iron: 1.1 mg
calcium: 176 mg

kiwifruit, melon, and passion fruit smoothie

This is a deliciously sweet, yet refreshing drink. If you cannot find passion fruit juice try using pineapple juice instead. This smoothie is beneficial after most exercise, particularly extra-energy, endurance, and muscular strength activities, when muscle glycogen stores are often quickly used up.

¼ watermelon, about 10 oz flesh
2 kiwifruit
¾ cup passion fruit juice

Remove and discard the seeds from the watermelon and dice the flesh. Put it in a freezer container and freeze for at least 2 hours or overnight. Peel and roughly chop the kiwifruit and place them in a food processor or blender with the watermelon and the passion fruit juice and process until thick. Serve immediately. **Makes 1¾ cups; Serves 1**

Nutrition Notes

This smoothie is an excellent source of vitamins A, C, B1, B2, B6, copper, potassium, zinc, magnesium, and phosphorus and provides useful amounts of iron and calcium. Its wealth of nutrients makes it perfect after a wide range of exercise and sports.

Per serving

calories: 250
fat: 1.7 g
carbohydrate: 55 g
protein: 4.5 g
iron: 2.4 mg
calcium: 65 mg

banana and mango smoothie

Supplying good amounts of carbohydrate and potassium for nerve and muscle function, bananas are a popular snack among endurance athletes. They also contain a type of fiber, fructoligosaccharides (FOS), which encourages the growth of friendly lactobacilli bacteria in the gut. These help prevent the overgrowth of bad bacteria, which can cause health problems, such as digestive disorders.

1 ripe banana
1 ripe mango
¾ cup orange juice
¾ cup lowfat milk
3 tablespoons plain yogurt

Peel and slice the banana. Peel the mango, remove the pit, and cut the flesh into even-size pieces. Put the banana, mango, orange juice, milk, and yogurt in a food processor or blender and process until smooth. Pour into 2 glasses, add a few ice cubes to each glass if desired, and drink immediately. **Makes 2 cups; Serves 2**

Nutrition Notes

This smoothie is an excellent source of vitamins A, C, B1, B2, B6, B12, folic acid, calcium, potassium, magnesium, and phosphorus.

Per serving

calories: 190
fat: 3 g
carbohydrate: 37 g
protein: 6 g
iron: 0.95 mg
calcium: 155 mg

strawberry and pineapple smoothie

Like many smoothies, this one is a great way of restoring energy after exercise, when solid food may not appeal. It contains a high level of calcium, which is essential for healthy bones, helps to maintain normal blood pressure and plays a role in nerve transmission, muscle contraction, and blood clotting—all of which are crucial bodily functions for athletes.

1 cup strawberries
⅔ cup pineapple juice
⅔ cup strawberry yogurt

Wash, hull and roughly chop the strawberries, then place them in a freezer container and freeze for at least 2 hours or overnight. Place the frozen strawberries, pineapple juice, and yogurt in a food processor or blender and process until smooth. Pour into a glass, add a couple of ice cubes, decorate with strawberries, if desired, and drink immediately. **Makes 1¾ cups; Serves 1**

Nutrition Notes

This smoothie is an excellent source of vitamins C, B2, B6, folic acid, calcium, zinc, magnesium, and phosphorus.

Per serving

calories: 260
fat: 4.5 g
carbohydrate: 48 g
protein: 9 g
iron: 0.9 mg
calcium: 276 mg

dried fruit salad smoothie

This excellent smoothie allows athletes to refuel and increase their energy levels after endurance activities and extra-energy sports, which can leave people feeling drained and hungry. Dried fruit provides a source of iron, so this is a good choice for those who are at risk of iron deficiency and those practicing impact sports.

¾ cup dried fruit salad
1¾ cups apple juice, more if necessary
¾ cup whole milk yogurt

Roughly chop the fruit and place it in a large bowl. Pour the apple juice over it, cover the bowl, and allow to stand overnight. Put the dried fruit salad and apple juice in a food processor or blender, add the yogurt, and process until smooth, adding a little more apple juice if necessary. Pour into 2 glasses, add a couple of ice cubes, if desired, and serve immediately. **Makes 1¾ cups; Serves 2**

Nutrition Notes

This smoothie is an excellent source of vitamins A, C, B2, B6, B12, calcium, potassium, magnesium, and phosphorus and also provides useful amounts of iron.

Per serving

calories: 280
fat: 8 g
carbohydrate: 48 g
protein: 7 g
iron: 2.3 mg
calcium: 200 mg

glossary

Antioxidant: A compound that protects cells against the damaging effects of free radicals. Vitamins C, E, beta-carotene and selenium, and many of the phytochemicals found in fruit and vegetables act as antioxidants.

Carbohydrate: A primary energy fuel for the body.

Enzyme: A protein that speeds up chemical reactions and processes in the body.

Ergogenic aid: A substance that is capable of enhancing work performance.

Essential fatty acids: These are polyunsaturated fatty acids, which cannot be made by the body and so must be supplied by food. The main sources of essential fatty acids (also called linoleic and linolenic acids) are olive and vegetable oils, fish oils, polyunsaturated margarine, and nuts.

Fiber: Also called non-starch polysaccharides (NSP), this is the word used to describe several different compounds found in the cell walls of all plants. The body cannot digest fiber but it still plays an important role in our health. Fiber can be divided into two groups—see Soluble fiber and Insoluble fiber.

Free radicals: These are highly reactive molecules which cause damage to cell walls and DNA (the genetic material found within cells). They are believed to be involved in the development of heart disease, some cancers, and

premature aging. Free radicals are produced naturally but certain factors such as smoking, pollution, and exposure to sunlight can accelerate their production.

Fructoligosaccharides (FOS): A type of fiber that escapes the digestive process and is fermented by the bacteria in the gut. FOS encourage the growth of "friendly" lactobacilli bacteria in the gut.

Glycemic index (GI): A measure of how quickly carbohydrate is turned into blood glucose. Foods with a high GI are quickly broken down and provide a fast energy fix, while those with a low GI are absorbed more slowly and steadily into the blood. Unfortunately, there is no easy way to tell what the GI of a food is. Some sugars have a high GI and others a low GI. Some complex carbohydrates have a low GI whereas others have a higher GI. Foods that have a low glycemic index include beans, lentils, apples, pears, pasta, dried apricots, and whole wheat cereals. Foods with a high glycemic index include honey, baked potatoes, glucose, white rice, bagels, and watermelons.

Glycogen: The main carbohydrate store in the body, stored mainly in the liver and muscles.

Insoluble fiber: Found in wholegrain cereals, legumes, fruit and vegetables, insoluble fiber increases stool bulk and speeds the passage of waste material through the body. It helps prevent constipation, hemorrhoids, diverticular disease and may protect against bowel cancer.

Macronutrients: Nutrients that are present in foods in large quantities; they include fats, proteins, and carbohydrates.

Micronutrients: Nutrients that are present in foods in small quantities; they include vitamins and minerals.

Minerals: Inorganic substances that perform a wide range of vital functions throughout the body.

Phytochemicals: Naturally occurring compounds that plants produce to protect themselves against bacteria, viruses, and fungi. They are not nutrients in the true sense of the word because they are not essential in the diet, but they are biologically active and there is a growing amount of evidence to suggest that they can help protect against various types of cancer, heart disease, and chronic degenerative diseases like cataracts and arthritis.

Soluble fiber: This is found in oats, beans and lentils, fruit and vegetables and can help reduce high blood cholesterol levels and control blood sugar levels by slowing down the absorption of sugar.

Vitamins: A group of compounds, required in minute amounts, but essential for good health. There are about 20 vitamins, most of which cannot be made by the body so must be obtained from the diet. Each vitamin performs one or several essential functions. The body can store some vitamins (A, D, E, K, and B12); the rest need to be provided regularly by diet.

index

Acknowledgments

The author and publisher would like to thank PPL (tel: 01159
608646, www.superjuicer.co.uk) for the loan of the Superjuicer,
and Magimix for the loan of Le Duo juicer.

Executive Editor Nicky Hill
Editor Charlotte Wilson
Design Manager Tokiko Morishima
Design 'OME Design
Production Controller Nosheen Shar
Photographer Karen Thomas
Home Economist David Morgan
Stylist Angela Swaffield
Illustrations Line + Line